I Am a Refugee

FINDING HOME AGAIN IN AMERICA

Mirsada Kadiric

ISBN: 1983932019
ISBN 13: 9781983932014

The world will not be destroyed by those who do evil,
but by those who watch them without doing anything.
—Albert Einstein, the world's most famous refugee

I dedicate this book first and foremost to my mother, the toughest refugee I have ever known. Mom, without your courage, your survival skills, and your nurturing ways, I wouldn't be here today, writing this book. Not only did you give life to me, but you continue to breathe life into me to this day. And I can only wish to be half the woman you are in my lifetime. Mom, you are my hero and my ultimate inspiration for life.

I also dedicate this book to all of the refugees forced to wander the world today. May you find, as I did, a place that will welcome you, and a place you can call home again.

Table of Contents

Opening Thoughts

MERRIAM-WEBSTER DEFINES THE WORD "REFUGEE" as "a person who flees to a foreign country to escape danger or persecution." I find in today's society there is a lot of confusion around the word refugee. First, refugees are just lumped into the broader "immigrant" bucket without a context. Refugees do not leave their country of birth by free will, they are forced to leave, and it is a life or death situation they are faced with. Second, adding to the confusion is the association with various religious backgrounds which are complex and hard to define with certainty. And as part of this "refugee confusion", fear of refugees has spread around the globe. Meanwhile, according to the UN Refugee Agency (UNHCR), there are roughly more than sixty-five million forcibly displaced people worldwide; twenty-two million of them are refugees in various countries, and half of them are children under the age of eighteen. Back in 1992, I was one of those kids.

At age ten, I held my mother's hand as we were forced to flee our home in Bosnia in search for a new place we could call home again. Our refugee journey was long. We jumped from country to country until we were finally given a chance at a new life here in the United States, in the Greater Cincinnati area. At that time, the US government was giving Bosnian war refugees a chance to become permanent residents, with the opportunity to become citizens five years later. And my mother and I are thankful every day that they did. Without the assistance from the United States, who knows where we would be today. Chances are we wouldn't even be alive. Instead, we are fully integrated, self-sufficient, and productive citizens of this great nation, and we feel connected to the Greater Cincinnati community.

Given my personal story of coming to this country as a refugee and becoming a proud American citizen, I found it important to speak up about it. Today we are faced with one of the greatest refugee crises in history. And in the future, it's estimated that the number of people fleeing their homelands will only increase exponentially due to various geopolitical factors. With this book, I wanted to give a face to what the word refugee ultimately means: people forced to leave their homes, with no say in the matter, looking for a way to survive, like any other human being would if faced with a similar situation.

Being a refugee is not a choice. Yet, being a refugee can be looked down upon. Many assume you're looking for a free handout. Others are afraid you may harm them. It is difficult to relate to a refugee unless you've personally experienced it. Having your home taken away from you, being ripped apart from your community, and then transplanted into a foreign culture, custom, and language where you have very little time to adjust and move on with your life. All you want is a roof over your head without the fear of being killed, and you would give your best to any place that would give you this opportunity. Refugees are survivors. They are people; human beings looking for peace from their fellow human beings.

As the political rhetoric started to heat up ahead of the 2016 US presidential election, I started to reflect on my life and express it in writing. As a beginning to my refugee story, I want to open with a reflection I've written, appropriately titled "My World Is Your World."

My World Is Your World

THIS WORLD IS PLENTY BIG for all of us to share, and isolationism will never work for anyone. No one place in this world has everything it needs to sustain itself. That's why the world is round—it has no beginning or end; we are all in the midst of it. I need you just as much as you need me. We need each other to survive and to thrive.

It boggles my mind when we treat life so carelessly! Once a life is gone, it's gone forever! We all have someone in our lives we wish we could bring back…to touch them, hug them, kiss them…to hear them speak once again, exchange stories with them, and laugh with them.

Why can't we cherish life as the most precious thing given to us? Without life nothing else would be possible—the things we've owned, the accolades we've received, and even the good memories we've made. Let's remind ourselves of the preciousness of life, of the similarities between us, and of the one place we all have in common: this world of ours!

Acknowledgements

To the love of my life, Dr. Richard Larry Gaston, thank you for giving me the courage to put my story out there for the rest of the world to see. Without your reassurance and persistent pressure, this book wouldn't exist today. I also thank you for all the precious time you put into reviewing this book, providing me with constructive feedback, and helping me make it as impactful as it can be. You are an amazing human being, and I'm the luckiest woman on this planet to have you as my partner for life!

CHAPTER 1

Life Is But a Daring Adventure

FOR ME, BEING A FIRSTBORN child and the first grandchild on both sides of the family meant being showered with love, attention, and lots of presents. To say I was spoiled would be an understatement. My maternal grandmother still tells the story of coming to visit me daily. She'd send Grandpa off to work, prepare for the forty-five-minute bus ride to my house, spend a few hours playing with me, and then she'd leave in time to be home to greet him when he returned from work. She also says now that's the reason why I am willing to travel all the way from America to come visit her every year.

One of my biggest fans was, of course, my dad. He used to tell me that if my mother were to line up ten boys in front of him, he would still pull me out of the lineup as his favorite.

Sports analogies were something he was good at, and early on in my life, he introduced me to his passion for his favorite sport, soccer (or, as I like to refer to it, the original football). I remember watching games with him, screaming at the top of my lungs at the television, something I've still been known to do.

For my fourth birthday, after I'd begged them for months, my parents finally decided to get me a bike. But what was supposed to have been a happy event turned into crocodile tears. I was devastated that they'd chosen to get me a "little-girl bike" (in my own words), complete with training wheels. How dare they? I was a big girl now! Never wanting to disappoint me, my father rushed back into town and came back with a "big-girl bike," a baby-blue Pony with no training wheels. Even with the seat completely lowered, I still couldn't reach the pedals. But that wasn't going to stop me. I was determined to learn how to ride that bike, standing up or sitting down.

I started out by placing a cushion on the grooved middle part of the frame and straddling the bike while sitting on the cushion. I would hold on to the handlebars, lift my feet off the ground, and let the bike roll down the small incline of our driveway. I repeated that over and over again, days at a time, until I was brave enough one day to stand with my left foot on one pedal while balancing myself with my right foot on the frame, and I rolled down that same incline. A few weeks later, I felt confident enough to put my other foot on the other pedal, and I just started pedaling. I pedaled that bike in a standing position for a whole year until I was tall enough to sit down and pedal. To say I'm stubborn would be an understatement—just ask my mother.

That same stubbornness led me to teach myself how to swim as well. A small river, the Sana, ran through the town of Prijedor, about twenty minutes' walking distance from our house. One day, I decided to go to the river with one of my cousins, Senada, who was just a few days younger than I. Being the smart little girl I was, I made sure I packed us a snack (the whole fresh loaf of bread my grandmother had made that morning, coupled with some chicken pâté, one of my favorite combinations), grabbed a towel, and off we went. Swimming was a multistep learning process, just like biking. I started out by pinching my nose and putting my head under water while standing up. I eventually let my feet go and just figured out how to stay afloat by wiggling around a lot. My mother was in a panic when she came home to a note that said I'd gone swimming. I would give my mother lots of moments of panic in my lifetime, from being sandwiched between two cars while on my bike to my first car accident at age sixteen.

My father didn't fare much better when it came to worrying about me. He took me to the emergency room many times. Since he worked at the hospital as part of the ambulance crew, eventually everyone got to know my name there too. Even a small pinky sprain got an x-ray, just in case. But one day I gave him a scare he would never forget. I was playing with my friends across the street from our house, and we decided it was a good idea to climb up and walk on top of a haystack, barefoot. What we didn't realize was that the hay was stacked on a wooden frame that was barely held together with some rusty old nails. And just like that, I stepped with full force on a five-inch nail that punctured my entire foot.

My father was outside working on his car when he heard my scream. He would later tell me that the scream sounded like nothing short of someone dying, and he recognized my voice. Dropping everything to the ground, he ran across the street as fast as he could, only to find me in a pool of blood. He immediately took off his shirt, wrapped it around my foot, and picked me up off the ground. We proceeded to make another ER trip.

My father was a hero in my big brown eyes. At six feet four, he towered over me. His thick, dark, wavy hair, coupled with his bushy black eyebrows, made for a stern face. Yet he would always crack a smile when he looked at me. Even as we sat in the ER, waiting for my foot to be made whole again, he smiled as he observed my battered and bruised legs (my trademark look from all the adventures I got myself into as a child). He used to say that he didn't know if I would even have legs to stand on when I got older, considering how much I abused them.

Even though my father never had any other children, he had in me the perfect child: a sweet little girl with the rambunctiousness of a boy. But that was not all. Once I started school, I was also the best student, one of the qualities my father was most proud of.

My dad's protective grip and adoring gaze.

Being an only child, I wanted to be around other children, and I always wished for a brother or a sister. Going to school would give me the opportunity to be around other children, and I couldn't wait to start. But long before that, I learned simple arithmetic by playing cards with my grandfather. I was the only child in school who could add and subtract well before I could write my name. Maybe that is why

I've loved numbers all my life. But numbers weren't the only thing I was good at. Being so determined to figure out everything on my own, I was eager to learn anything that was thrown my way, so much so that I was one of the top two students in my class. I was also in close competition with one of my boy classmates to be the class president, and I was determined to beat him every time.

Outside of the classroom, I competed with my boy cousins, whom I preferred to play with. (Dolls were for the girly girls; I never owned a doll, nor did I want to.) Whether the contest was a climb dare, stealing eggs from chicken coops, or sledding down a hill the fastest, I always wanted to win. This competitive nature has followed me into my adulthood.

Me playing in the dirt in the pretty dress
my mother picked out for the day.

My fourth-grade class in Bosnia.

There's nothing more precious than childhood, and mine was a typical one: sweet and innocent, daring and fun, but most importantly filled with lots of love. I had not a care in the world. My days were filled with lots of laughter, and I daydreamed of what life would be like when I grew up. Being a daddy's girl, I naturally looked up to my father and wanted to be just like him. One day, I thought, I too would work in a hospital and help heal people. I've carried that compassion for others all through my life, and I credit that to my father. People who knew him best have told me that he was a special kind of man, that he didn't have a selfish bone in his body, and that he would help others before he helped himself. In a society ravaged by selfish acts, I'm even prouder to be my father's daughter. I wish I'd had more time to learn from him, to emulate him, to make him proud. But our time was cut short when I was just ten years old.

CHAPTER 2

The Day I Last Saw My Father

It was a Sunday in July; I still remember it as clear as day. Sundays meant family time around a good, home-cooked meal. My father's parents lived with us, and my grandmother was preparing the traditional Bosnian dish known as pita—not the flatbread common in the Mediterranean and Middle East, but a thin, flaky, pastry-like dough filled with a savory goodness and baked to perfection. On that day, she was making my dad's favorite pita called *burek*, which meant the filling was made up of seasoned ground beef. Given my innate curiosity and thirst for knowledge, I naturally wanted to help my grandmother and learn how to make pita as well. And that day, she let me make the pita as independently as possible. After the baking process was done, I was quite impressed by my creation and couldn't wait for my father to try it.

He was just a short distance away from our house, doing what he so frequently did—helping someone. In this case, he was helping fix one of his cousin's cars. When he arrived back home, he was accompanied by his cousin Midho, whom he'd invited to have family dinner with us. Normally we'd have been eating outside, as we often did in the summer when the heat made it too uncomfortable in the house (air conditioning was something I didn't learn about until I got to the United States). However, the light drizzle that day forced us to eat on the covered porch instead. My father devoured the *burek* I made and raved that it was the best meal he'd ever had in his life. I just sat there watching him eat, beaming from ear to ear. Nothing satisfied me more than his approval, even though I could do no wrong in his eyes, and that day was a big win in my book.

Suddenly, we were startled by a large truck, similar to a big U-Haul, that roared down the street and came to an abrupt stop right in front of our driveway. In an instant, roughly fifty heavily armed men in uniforms surrounded our house and screamed for us to come out with our hands in the air. As we stood there in the rain, the one who appeared to be the leader of the pack stepped forward with a piece of paper in his hand and asked if this was the house of Ratib Kadiric.

My father replied, "Yes, it is."

"And which one of you is him?" the man asked.

"That's me, my brother."

"Don't call me your brother," the man shot back angrily, and told him to come forward.

Two of the armed men hurried toward my father, grabbed him by his arms, and pressed him against our fence. While

one of the men held his arms behind his back, the other proceeded to pat him down. The whole time, my father's eyes
were focused on me, and he wore a faint smile, one that only
I could bring out of him. My big eyes were wide open, I was
scared, and I wanted to ask so many questions. But in that
moment I couldn't help but smile back at him.

My family and I could see the leader asking my father
some questions, but we couldn't hear the conversation. Then
the leader asked Midho who he was, and after learning he
was my father's cousin, he said, "Get over here. You're coming
with us too."

Two other armed men quickly patted him down as well
and proceeded to take both of them to the truck. Midho went
in first. Before my father stepped into the back of the truck,
he looked at us one more time, paused, made eye contact with
me, smiled, and winked. That was the last time I would see
my father's face. To this day, that image of him is inked in
my brain.

The rest of the armed men piled back inside the truck,
turned on the loud diesel engine, and roared away from our
house. My grandparents, mom, and I slowly lowered our
hands, and I immediately jumped into my mother's arms,
crying. She was visibly shaken. Nobody said a word as we
went back onto the porch. I could see my grandmother crying
too, and my grandfather was deep in thought.

A short while later, Midho came running down our driveway. He was out of breath and had fear in his eyes. Without
sitting down (he wanted to get back to his parents' house as

quickly as possible), he briefly explained what had happened on the truck. The armed men had a list of men's names, and they were going house to house, collecting the men on their list. Roughly ten others were on the truck when they picked up my father. After they got Midho's name, they asked him what he did for a living. He told them he was studying biology at a university in a neighboring town and was back home for the summer. The men decided that since his name wasn't on the list, they had no need for him at that time. They yelled to the driver to stop the truck and forced Midho to jump off—but not before he'd gathered that they were taking all the men on that truck to Keraterm, an old abandoned factory in town.

During the early days of 1992, the Yugoslav People's Army had started to gather in town ahead of the major local elections that ultimately led to Bosnia becoming its own republic and splitting from Yugoslavia (originally, the nation of Yugoslavia was made up of five different countries: Slovenia, Croatia, Bosnia-Herzegovina, Serbia, and Montenegro). The army promised that they were there just to protect us, but word had spread that "camps" were set up in a few of the abandoned factories, where they took people for questioning regarding their political affiliations and religious backgrounds. My family was of Muslim ancestry, dating back to the Ottoman Empire in the fifteenth century, but my parents didn't actively practice the religion. I would later learn that my father was one of the key young political voices in town, one of the social democrats who opposed the old Yugoslavian communist governance and who were suspected and propagated of posing the threat of a "Muslim uprising."

My mother knew exactly where Keraterm was, so she got up before sunrise, made some breakfast, hopped on her moped, and rode into town, hoping to visit with my father. I stayed back with my grandparents, and we eagerly awaited her return. When she got back, we could see how shaken she was, even though she tried to hide it. She told us our little city had started to change dramatically, with army checkpoints set up throughout, monitoring the traffic in and out of the city.

Once she finally made it to Keraterm, she was greeted at the gate by some of my father's former friends and colleagues. They were of Serbian origin, Orthodox Christians who made up the other half of our town's population. They'd always lived in harmony with the Muslim population until political propaganda began to divide us. The imagined threat of a Muslim takeover forced them to take a side, and they sided with the army as a way to protect themselves.

As my mother pleaded to see my father, they reassured her that he was in safe hands with them. They told her not to worry and to return home. They did not even accept the food she had brought, saying they had given him plenty. My mother made that trip a few more times before she was told she was no longer allowed through the checkpoints. Each time she went, she was turned away by those same gatekeepers.

Mom and Dad in the early days of their love.

CHAPTER 3

When Your Home Is No Longer Yours

IT WASN'T LONG AFTER MY father was taken away that we truly started to feel what it was like living in a war zone. The nights were the worst. The valley in which our town was situated was surrounded by army tanks on top of the hills, and the tanks actively bombed during the nighttime. A loud boom from the tanks would be followed by lots of fiery sounds of machine guns in the distance. It was like listening to a fireworks exhibition—the big explosion that leaves everyone in awe, followed by the little firecrackers that add color commentary to the show. Watching fireworks still brings back memories of war for me.

We would hide in neighbors' basements at night (our home didn't have one), trying to avoid a stray bomb hitting our home. Word on the street was that the army was advancing at night, one home at a time, clearing it of its inhabitants; some were killed on the spot, especially if they were male, while others were taken into concentration camps. If there was any attempt to show resistance, it was met with armed force. The empty homes were then usually set on fire or bombed until they resembled nothing but a pile of rubble.

During the day, armed soldiers went door to door and took any valuables from the houses that were still inhabited. I remember the day they visited our home. They came in and asked for the keys to my dad's car. As we sat inside, we saw them drive away with the car and pack their trailer with some of my grandmother's furniture and even my beloved blue Pony bike. I let out a scream as I saw them taking the bike, but my mother quickly hushed me and told me to keep quiet, reassuring me that she'd buy me a new one.

My mother was worried and knew that the day we would be forced to leave our home was fast approaching. In preparation for that day, I saw her pack a large tote with as many pieces of our underwear as she could, our few family photos, and some crackers. I also saw her take all her gold jewelry, including her wedding ring, and seal it in a plastic bag. Inside that bag she also put the little cash she had on hand.

That same day, she cut my hair into a short crew-cut style and did the same to her own hair. And even though it was the middle of summer, she laid out three layers of clothes, including a winter jacket, which she instructed me to put on if we were told to leave the house. As she was doing all this, she explained that we must do whatever it took to not stand out in the crowd. I didn't fully understand her then, but later on I came to realize she did all that to protect us from being victims of rape. Further, the extra layers of clothing came in handy while sleeping on concrete floors.

A few days later, we were finally forced to leave our home. An unmarked vehicle with loudspeakers mounted on top drove slowly through our town, announcing that this was our final notice to leave, and gave us specific instructions about which meeting point we were to go to. They warned us that we only had two hours to leave, or we'd face grim consequences. Immediately, my mother rushed me to get dressed and grabbed the bag she'd packed. By this time, my grandfather had already been taken away during one of the raids. Yet, my grandmother was refusing to leave and argued with my mom that we needed to pack as many belongings with us as we could. This was no time for worrying about belongings, my mother understood it, and with tears in her eyes told my grandmother that we needed to leave, whether she wanted to come with us or not. She then turned to me, put her hands around my face, and told me that from this point forward it was going to be just her and I and that she needed me to follow her lead.

Up until this point, my mother's relationship with me was a nurturing one. Even though she worked full-time (not a common occurrence in Bosnia at that time), she was the one who made sure I was fed at all times, had clean clothes to wear, and comforted me in times of need. She was never too tired to do anything for me, and always put others' needs before hers. This is true to this day. But in that moment as we were getting ready to leave our home, I saw a fighter and a leader in her. Before that, I reserved that role for my dad whom I idolized. I was struck by my mom's seriousness and it was instantly clear to me that she was now in charge.

A long line of women and children were making their way down the street. They carried a big white sheet as a flag signaling our surrender, and we joined them. I saw some cousins and former schoolmates whom I hadn't seen since our last school day before the summer break. We exchanged brief smiles but held on to our mothers' hands and kept quiet with the adults.

Just as we rounded the corner from our house, my mother was stopped by one of the armed soldiers passing by. He pointed the gun at her and asked if she had any valuables on her. Prepared for this moment, my mother pulled out the plastic bag with her jewelry and cash in it and quickly handed it over to him. She gripped my hand tightly while we waited for him to inspect the bag. Satisfied with the contents, he motioned with the gun for us to continue on with the group.

As we made our way down the street, something we hadn't done since the nighttime bombings had started, we could finally see the extent of the damage that had been done. We passed the house where Elvis, my neighbor and good friend, had lived with his grandfather. I saw his bloody, lifeless body lying out on the driveway. A short distance from him laid his grandfather. Memories of us playing and sharing meals together flashed before my eyes, and I started to tear up. Why did they have to kill Elvis?

I looked up at my mother, distraught. She gripped my hand and motioned me not to make a noise. I was scared! For the first time, my ten-year-old mind could finally grasp that we were in a life-or-death situation. Everywhere we looked, male bodies lay on the sides of the street. Some weren't yet dead; we could hear them gasping for air, but we couldn't help. And it being in the middle of summer, the heat made the smell of death and dried blood even more unbearable, forcing me to breathe through my mouth.

About an hour later, we made it to the meeting point. Four big buses were waiting on us. The soldiers made note of our names, and then we were instructed to board. With no knowledge of our destination, we sat in silent fear as the buses took off. A short while later, the buses slowed, and we could finally make out our destination point, where armed soldiers waited to let us in. We were on the outskirts of a small neighboring town called Trnopolje, home to another old abandoned factory, now surrounded by barbed-wire fence.

As we made our way through the gate, we could see hundreds of people already inside—men, women, and children—most of them sitting on the bare ground, surrounded by armed soldiers. Soon we joined the masses, awaiting our next instructions. My mother recognized some of the faces, but most of us remained silent and did not interact with one another, trying not to attract the soldiers' attention. We'd heard of these concentration camps being set up throughout town, and now we were inside one ourselves.

As night approached, the soldiers sent groups of people into their designated spaces. We were put inside a small room full of women and children, with nothing but a few pieces of cardboard on the ground. My mother found a small space for us, sat down against the wall, and told me to put my head on her lap and go to sleep. I was tired, but I was also hungry, and it was hard to get comfortable on the concrete floor. The women whispered to one another, trying to figure out what was going to happen to us next. Some of them had overheard the soldiers talking about temporary imprisonment for women, and everyone was hopeful we would be released soon, but nobody could really sleep.

The quiet of the night was often interrupted by random gunshots. And every night, we heard the soldiers' raucous singing and laughing. Their boozy nights were every woman's worst nightmare and our greatest fear while in the camp. They would shine flashlights into the rooms of women and children, handpick the ones they thought were the prettiest, and take them away.

Later, we would hear those women and girls scream over the soldiers' boisterous laughs as they ripped off their clothes and gang raped them repeatedly throughout the night. Some never made it out alive, while others were scarred for life. My mother never slept through the night, and she always made sure we avoided the soldiers as much as possible, which helped us remain unscathed while in the camp.

We had no running water, no food, and the heat was unbearable, but my mother insisted that we keep our layers of clothing on. She gave me a cracker here and there, and made the trek to the groundwater pump to get us a fresh bottle of water every day.

We spent only five days in the camp, but it felt like an eternity. On the fifth day, the soldiers gathered all the women and children and instructed us to board big U-Haul–like trucks like the one that had taken my dad away, which were waiting in the courtyard. As the trucks took off, we once again had no knowledge of our destination, and this time no windows to show us where we were going. The fear was overwhelming, and most of the women and children were crying. I sat in my mom's lap while she remained stone faced and kept whispering to me to remain quiet.

The trucks came to an abrupt stop, the engines were shut off, and we heard the soldiers coming around. Suddenly the doors opened, and the soldiers started shouting at us to get out. Panic set in. People started trampling each other. My mother gripped my hand once again. We stood up and made our way off the truck. She jumped off first, and I leapt into her arms. We were in the middle of a forest somewhere. The soldiers shouted that we were free to go, and they pointed away from the trucks. We started walking. At last, we were free again.

CHAPTER 4

Freedom Is Not Easy to Come By

OUR FREEDOM CAME AT A really high price. As we walked away from the trucks, the soldiers opened fire behind us. Panic set in again, but this time in a much direr way. Everyone was pushing and shoving, screaming, and running as fast as possible. My mother never let go of my hand. It was as if we were glued together. Her fast pace was tough for my short legs to keep up with. At times it felt as if she were dragging me with such force that my feet were bouncing off the ground.

It is difficult to say how many people lost their lives that day in the forest. My mother and I never once stopped to look back; her sole focus was on keeping the two of us alive. As we marched through the forest, the sounds of the weapons subsided, and we began to see light peeking through the last line of trees. At this point, nobody was near us. We were walking so fast that we'd put quite a bit of distance between us and the rest of the group. That was just fine by my mother. Fewer people meant less suspicion and less chance of being killed.

Once at the edge of the forest, my mother slowed down to check the surroundings, trying to determine where we were. With no road signs in immediate sight, it was clear that we were on top of a mountain, looking down into the valley of a city. The road in front of us was paved and extremely steep. We continued to march. The pace was still too fast for me, but I knew better than to complain. I stayed silent as I held tightly to my mother's hand.

Then it finally appeared: the first road sign, which indicated that we were in the vicinity of Vlašić, a mountain just outside of the city of Travnik and a three-hour drive from my hometown. We had never been to Travnik before, but my mother had heard rumors in the concentration camp that it was the closest city under the control of the newly formed Bosnian Liberation Army, which was made up of Muslims and thus was a safe place for us. The road sign also indicated that we had thirty kilometers (roughly eighteen miles) to go, which was not welcome information to our malnourished and dehydrated bodies. Nonetheless, my mother kept pressing on.

As we made our descent, we started to notice signs of life as well. Homes were scattered throughout the side of the mountain, and one just happened to be footsteps away from the main road. A woman was outside washing clothes by hand, and my mother made a brave decision to approach her. The woman greeted us politely, even smiled at me. She was clearly startled, but she could also tell that we were in desperate need. Immediately she offered us water, which my mother hastily accepted. She confirmed with the woman that we were indeed by Vlašić and on the right path toward Travnik. We took a few more sips of water, thanked her, and off we went again. My mother's pace slowed a bit. Perhaps she felt she could relax for a moment, knowing that we were closer to safety, but perhaps she herself was finally showing signs of fatigue.

While it felt like a lifetime, roughly three hours later, we finally made it to the Bosnian Liberation Army checkpoint into the city of Travnik. Exhausted and hungry, we followed one of the soldiers to the refugee camp, which was set up inside a high school gymnasium. Once there, we realized that we weren't alone on this journey. Thousands of old hospital-like beds were squeezed into neat rows, mostly occupied by women and children.

My mother was spotted by an elderly lady who happened to be her aunt Sida, the wife of her father's brother. After a few hugs and tears, she escorted us to a bed next to hers, where she made space for my mother and me to lie down. That was the first night in a week that my mother finally got some sleep. But the next day was pure torture. Our bodies, having come off an adrenaline rush, finally showed signs of wear and tear from the fast-paced, eighteen-plus-mile walk from the day before. Neither one of us could step on our feet without excruciating pain.

Aunt Sida brought us some soup and a few pieces of bread (the only food available at the refugee camp), our first meal of the week. The day after, while we were still stiff, we were able to walk with much less pain. My mother left me in the care of Aunt Sida, the first time she'd taken her eyes off me in a week, in search of a way to communicate with the world outside of Bosnia.

My mother had two brothers and my father three, all of whom lived outside of Bosnia at that time. They'd been working and making a living elsewhere prior to the war breaking out. This was the norm back then—men left their families to find better employment opportunities in western parts of Europe. My mother was hopeful that she could get in touch with relatives to let them know that we were alive. And sure enough, when she came back to the camp, she told me that she'd been able to communicate with my dad's brother Abaz, who lived in Switzerland. He'd given her specific instructions to talk to one of the local taxi drivers who were now making a living by smuggling people out of the country. My uncle would pay the taxi once we arrived at a predetermined location, where he would be waiting for us. Arrangements were made. In three days a taxi would take us to the city of Ploče, which was located in the neighboring country of Croatia. My uncle would be waiting for us with his vehicle, and we would officially be out of the Bosnian war zone.

The taxi picked us up late at night. Smuggling people out of the country was done only at night, traveling off the beaten path, doing everything you could to remain invisible to the enemy army. In the taxi with us was my paternal grandmother who'd caught up after we'd lost track of her when we were in the concentration camp. Once we left our home, she stayed behind and managed to pack four large plastic bags of personal belongings that she dragged out of the house with her. That proved to be fruitless once she arrived to the meeting point where soldiers took everything away before they forced her onto the bus to the same concentration camp my mother and I were taken to. A former neighbor of ours was also in the taxi with us, whose son lived in Germany and was coming to pick her up in Ploče as well. We traveled the entire night, at times driving through forests and on makeshift paths created by the smugglers. We finally crossed the border as the sun was rising.

As we approached the meeting point, I spotted two of my uncles, Abaz and Hajrudin, eagerly awaiting us. Once outside the car, I ran toward them and hugged them as tightly as I could. There was no dry eye in sight, and everyone felt a sense of relief to finally be out of that nightmare. Much to my delight, my uncles, knowing we hadn't had a proper meal in days, had brought a trunk full of food. I can still see the bright yellow bananas and numerous bars of chocolate, two of my favorite foods. Needless to say, I gorged on both.

My uncles quickly paid the taxi driver, and we hurried away from the meeting point to avoid any unwanted attention from the local police. My uncle Hajrudin lived in Slovenia just outside of the capital, Ljubljana, which was the closest destination and our initial stop. The plan was to stay with him and his family for a few days, register with the local refugee agency to obtain temporary legal residency status, and ultimately find a place for us to live. The new school year was fast approaching, and my mother didn't want me to fall behind. She was eager for us to get back to some kind of normalcy as quickly as we could. But first she had to deal with the breakout of lice that we'd both contracted in the concentration camp, as well as a hospital stint for me, since my body was in the process of rejecting any kind of food after going for days without a proper meal.

A few weeks later, we settled into an apartment room that my mom's brother Hari rented from his former college roommate. The apartment was closer to the city and the school where I would attend fifth grade. The classes were taught in Serbo-Croatian, the official language of former Yugoslavia, of which Slovenia used to be a part. But I was also forced to learn Slovenian, a must if I was to continue my education in Slovenia. Aside from the very first day of school, when I took the wrong bus line home and ended up hours behind schedule, almost giving my mother a heart attack, life was fairly back to normal for me. I started to make a few friends in school, most of them also refugees from other parts of Bosnia, and everyone shared a similar backstory.

My fifth-grade class in Slovenia.

My mother still had no word of my father's whereabouts. Was he still alive? Would he make it out of Bosnia? The situation had worsened quickly, with full-out war unfolding on the ground, and very few people were able to make it out anymore. We had a little bit of Slovenian government monetary assistance, along with some food donations, but my mother was eager to get back to making money so we could live a bit more comfortably. Through my uncle Hari's various connections, she found some babysitting and housecleaning jobs, which she happily undertook. Regardless of what awaited us next, nothing could take away our feeling of freedom, our relief at having a roof over our heads and a bed to sleep in. Nobody could put a price tag on that.

CHAPTER 5

In Pursuit of a Better Life

LIFE, WHILE STABLE AND MOSTLY back to normal, was not easy for us in Slovenia. We rented a small room in someone else's apartment. While the landlord was a kind person, we did not enjoy the same freedoms as we had when we lived in our own home back in Bosnia. Our use of the bathroom, kitchen, and living room were all at the landlord's discretion. And while my mother found some work, none of it was steady or paid well. Slovenia, having recently also separated from former Yugoslavia, was struggling to find its way as an independent republic. There were limited funds for helping its own citizens, much less refugees.

Mom, me, and the little girl she babysat in
Slovenia (which made me jealous).

Two of my father's brothers lived in Switzerland, and after numerous discussions, we decided to get there as quickly as we could, ideally before I had to start sixth grade. Switzerland was one of the countries that every immigrant dreamed of entering. It was known for its superb social security and medical systems and high wages, not to mention the beautiful surroundings. But while moving to Switzerland was an easy decision to make, getting into the country would be next to impossible. At the time, the European Union did not exist, and each country strictly controlled its borders to protect itself from criminal activities, as well as from illegal immigration. If my mother and I were to get into Switzerland, it was going to have to be under illegal circumstances.

Just like Bosnian taxi drivers were smuggling people out of the country, numerous other illegal immigration networks were set up in the area to help Bosnians get into the Western European countries that had the most resources to support us. I was still too young to understand it at the time; all I remember is my mom telling me one day that we were going to move to Switzerland to be closer to my other uncles and to have a chance at a better life.

I finished the fifth grade in Slovenia as an honor-roll student, speaking fluent Slovenian by the time I was done. Even the locals could not detect an accent when I spoke. One night during the summer of 1993, we packed up the few clothes we had accumulated while in Slovenia and waited for a car to pick us up and take us to the promised land. My mother didn't know what to expect, but just like the escape from Bosnia, this journey wasn't going to be an easy one.

A gentleman who refused to give us his real name picked us up at the designated time and place, took half of his hefty fee (the other half was to be paid upon arrival at our destination), and off we went. Slovenia borders Italy on the west, and we had to drive through northern Italy to get to Switzerland. Right before we got to the Italian passport-control checkpoint, the car turned off the highway, and we proceeded to an apartment community. Once there, the gentleman took us to an empty apartment, which was clearly part of the illegal immigration network as well, and told us to wait for his return. He gave no time estimate, and we had no idea where we were. I could sense my mother's panic. Here we were, all alone in an empty, unlocked apartment, with the last bit of money my mother had scraped up while working odd jobs in Slovenia, unsure what the next move was. Being the resourceful woman that she was, she propped a chair against the bedroom door and told me to be ready to jump out the window (we were only on the second floor) should things go wrong here.

I couldn't fight sleep any longer and dozed off while my mother guarded the door. She was unable to even close her worrying eyes. Much to our surprise, that same gentleman returned around two in the morning in another vehicle with another set of refugees, ready for us to cross the Italian border. He explained that we would not be crossing the border in the car. Instead, we would walk through the woods on foot to get to the other side of the border. Once in the woods, he showed us a clearing where he said we would have to cross as fast as we could, as he had been shot at there by border patrol agents several times before. This time, though, nobody was shooting, and as the sun began to rise again, we were officially in Italy. The same vehicle that had picked us up at the apartment was waiting for us at the border. We got in and drove for almost five hundred kilometers (roughly three hundred miles) to Switzerland.

We had to cross the border between Italy and Switzerland on foot and at night as well. Given that we had some time before dusk, we stopped at a rest area, got some snacks, and awaited further instructions from the driver. This time there were no woods to walk through. In this particular town, a tiny canal separated the two countries. It was protected by a large fence in which the smugglers had cut a hole. We had to climb through the hole, walk through the water, and meet them on the other side of the canal. I've been a little clumsy all my life, and I scraped my back on the fence as I climbed through that small hole. But aside from the little scratch on my back, my mother and I arrived safely inside the country of our dreams. The smuggler's vehicle awaited us and drove us to my uncle's address. Only once there could my mother breathe a sigh of relief. She happily paid the rest of the smuggler's fee, and we got a good night's sleep that night.

The next day, I woke up to my mother and my uncle establishing the story we would tell the Swiss immigration officials when we went to register at the refugee center. We knew that the refugee center did not turn away anyone, yet we couldn't readily reveal the extent of our illegal journey. We would simply say that we'd entered the country on foot, that nobody had checked us at the border, and, most importantly, that we had no home to go back to in Bosnia. And that was all true. We'd learned that our home—as a matter of fact, the entire suburb—had been leveled by the enemy army after we were forced to leave.

After we spent the weekend at my uncle's house, he drove us to the refugee center, which was located in the city of Basel, about an hour's drive from his house. Once there, he dropped us off with the guard, and we were on our own again.

The registration process went smoothly, and we were assigned to a room that was set up to house as many refugees as possible. Each room held about a hundred people in rows of tri-level twin-sized bunk beds. My mother and I got assigned to one of the beds on the third level. The climb alone was dizzying, and the space between the bed and the ceiling was quite small, even for me. I struggled to climb up the stairs the day after they vaccinated us, with several vaccines having been jabbed in my upper thigh. Both my mother and I had run-ins with the ceiling, scraping knees, heads, and backs until we got used to sleeping on the third level.

We spent roughly one week at the main refugee center, undergoing numerous questioning sessions, until we got word that we were officially being given temporary refugee status and would be transferred to another, smaller refugee center while awaiting a more permanent place to live.

The next refugee center was similar to the first, but it housed a much smaller population. A total of three floors, each with four main rooms. The sleeping quarters on the top two floors had the same tri-level bunk beds and housed roughly fifty refugees per room. The first floor had a communal area with a shared kitchen, bathrooms, and even a game room. Each family received a monthly stipend that they could spend as they wished, though mostly it was just enough for groceries. The main difference versus the first refugee center was that we were free to come and go as we wished, with only a late-night curfew in effect after midnight.

Mom with some of the refugee center crew at
a picnic the center organized for us.

Me with the rest of the refugee center crew at the picnic.

Summer was coming to an end quickly, and we knew that we would only be there temporarily while the local government officials looked for a more permanent place for us to live and for me to enroll in school. In the meantime, I befriended a girl from Bosnia, Emina, who just happened to be my age and had lived in a suburb of the same town I came from. Her family (mom, dad, and an older sister) grew close to my mom and me, and we acted like one big family. So when the day came to move us to a more permanent living space, they treated us as a family unit, and our two families were housed in adjoining bedrooms that shared an entrance to the main hallway.

My mother and I were in the smaller of the bedrooms that had its own door we could lock, but we had to walk through Emina's family's bedroom to be able to leave the premises, even to go to the bathroom. And that was not the worst part about this living space. We'd been transferred to an old office building that had been abandoned for years and was now infested with cockroaches.

It was a two-story building with a communal kitchen, laundry, and showers in the basement. A set of stairs separated the two floors, with the upper floor having the individual family bedrooms (roughly twelve of them, varying in shape and size, and none of them furnished, other than with one tri-level bunk bed per room), along with two communal sink/ bathroom areas. When we initially refused to accept this as our permanent living space, the local police showed up with their dogs, forced us into their vehicles, and dropped us off in front of the building with our keys to the doors, no further questions asked or answered. The only response my mother got from the social worker that day was that we could sleep in the building or sleep in the street.

We slept there the first night with our faces wrapped in towels so that the cockroaches would not get into our mouths and ears. The next day everyone got to work, cleaning the building from top to bottom, trying to make that place hospitable to people but not to cockroaches.

CHAPTER 6

All Is Great in Switzerland

WINNING THE WAR ON COCKROACHES was easy, but making that place feel like a home was going to take a long time. For one, the monthly living stipend we received was barely enough for food and basic necessities. And two, sharing the kitchen, laundry, and bathrooms with ten other families made for some highly unsanitary situations, ultimately prompting my mother to spearhead a committee to institute a weekly cleaning schedule, with each family sharing the cleaning duties for the whole building. What would typically be a chore turned into fun family cleaning nights, with music and laughter during the cleaning sessions, and everyone got their hands dirty. Reflecting on it now, I realize I probably get my cleaning obsession from those days. But most importantly, we finally had clean living conditions.

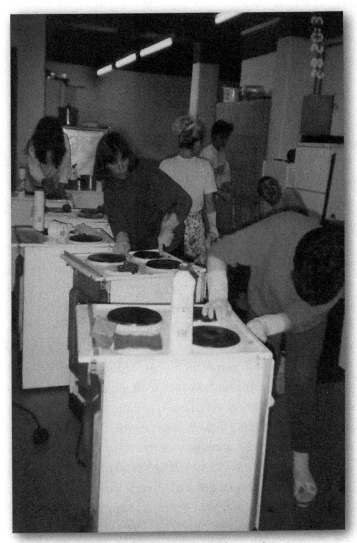

One of the family cleaning nights, with my
mom (center) leading the charge.

The next step was furnishing our rooms. Having a bed to sleep on was great, but with no place to put our few clothes, no couch to sit on, no table to eat at, and no desk for me to read and write at, it was hard to make ourselves comfortable. While we had no extra money for furniture, one of the greatest things about living in Switzerland at that time were "furniture disposal nights" every Tuesday. Because it was so expensive to dispose of furniture properly via the trash-removal companies, most people would set unwanted furniture out on the street at night in hopes that someone would take it by the following day so they didn't have to pay to have it removed. And that was exactly what we did. Walking around in groups for hours on end once it got dark, knowing where the best and richest streets were, we scored everything from couches to fully functioning TVs and dressers, among other things. It was like Christmas for us every Tuesday night. And everyone helped each other out. If we knew another family needed a table and we spotted one, we'd take it for them. Transporting it by hand was not easy, and it took a lot of time, but we laughed our way through the pain. Little by little, each of the families slowly furnished their tiny personal quarters. And nobody complained about having mismatched chairs or dinged-up tables.

As the days flew by, my mother was eager to earn some money so we could live a bit more comfortably. Given our temporary refugee status, she had no option to work legally in the country, so she looked for various odd jobs again that would pay her in cash. The biggest moneymaker was doing housecleaning work for the rich Swiss families, but my mother also went out into the fields during various harvest periods to pick strawberries and other farm-grown goods. Not only would she earn a little bit of money, but she could also get some free fresh produce for us as well. That job came at a high cost, though. She caught pneumonia one time after picking strawberries on a cold, rainy day, and lay ill in bed for days on end, with an extremely high fever.

We were ecstatic when she finally landed a job at a local five-star hotel as a housekeeper, with the agreement that she would be paid under the table, as they struggled to maintain a consistent labor force. While the work was really hard, my mother earned generous tips and made quite a decent living for us. She even saved up five hundred Swiss francs and splurged on a brand-new bike for my birthday. She was finally able to fulfill her promise to me the day they took my Pony in Bosnia.

At last, I was the proud owner of a brand-new bike again. I rode that thing everywhere. Nothing gave me more joy than being on that bike. It was a deep purple, almost the color of an eggplant, and shiny, with white tires that provided a great contrast. I was proud of my bike, and everyone noticed it—so much so that one morning I walked out to the bike stand in front of our building and discovered that someone had stolen it. I was once again devastated and broke out into tears. Our bedroom window was right above the bike stand. Hearing my crying, my mother peeked out, and she tried to console me. Filing a police report was useless, but I did so anyway. In the meantime, my mother got me another bike. This one wasn't as flashy, but it also wasn't as expensive. I was just happy to have a bike to take to school again.

School-wise, I was in a tough transitionary period. After the fifth grade, the Swiss school system divided the student population into three separate programs based on your performance (low, medium, and high). Those with the highest honors got to attend the progymnasium for four years (sixth through tenth grade), which ultimately meant you were on a trajectory to enter a university for an advanced degree down the road. While my transcripts from Bosnia and Slovenia indicated I qualified for the progymnasium program, my lack of German language proved problematic. Hence, I was enrolled temporarily into a fifth-grade repeat class alongside fellow immigrants, with the sole focus on learning the German language. While I'd been lucky enough to attend my native Serbo-Croatian–speaking school in Slovenia, finding one of those in Switzerland was not going to be possible. I needed to learn German—and learn it fast—so that I could continue on with my schooling.

Ultimately I spent eight months in that class, but I finally got to a point where my German was good enough for me to join the regular fifth-grade class to finish that school year. I was definitely the odd man out on campus, but my teacher liked me immediately and took me under his wing. Going against all rules, he even wrote to the school board personally to vouch for me and advise them to admit me to the highest school program, even though my German was still a work in progress.

Suffice it to say, once I officially started sixth grade a few months later, I had a target on my back from day one. The rest of the kids from my fifth-grade class who were also chosen to go to the highest school program felt I was unfairly given credit and did not deserve to be there. It did not help that I was the only kid who showed up with her mom on the first day of class. The children were pointing and laughing as my mother proudly held my hand, the same hand she'd held as we ran from gunfire in the Bosnian forest, while I stood there crying again.

Luckily, the first day was not a precursor to the remainder of the year. Even though some of my classmates (those who'd attended the last bit of fifth grade with me) questioned my admission to the progymnasium, the class was composed of the highest-honor students from various schools in town, so there was no group majority who ganged up against me. I slowly started to build alliances, especially since I had the smarts to compete with the rest of them. And with those alliances, my German started to improve dramatically as well.

I finally felt like my old self again! My grades were excellent, my teachers were impressed, and so were my classmates. Further, they all loved my story and where I came from. Everyone was curious to hear more about it, but even more so to try some of my mother's home cooking. I quickly bonded with Nicole and Livia, two locals who'd grown up together. They acted like sisters but proudly inducted me into their sisterhood.

At first I was shy and embarrassed about where I lived, and I never invited any of my friends over. During wintertime, when I couldn't ride my bike to school, I would wait for the streetcar to pass before I made my turn to walk toward my building. I never wanted anyone to know that I was living in the midst of an industrial zone, in a formerly cockroach-infested building, in a tiny room with random street furniture in it. I couldn't imagine the horror if one of my friends recognized a piece of her old furniture in our room. Yet Nicole and Livia were different. They truly made me feel like one of their own. I was regularly invited into their homes for dinner with their families, and I felt obligated to return the favor.

When the day came that they first visited me, my mother went to the park so we could have some privacy. All the shame I felt was blown away by their genuine reaction, intrigue, sympathy, and tears. They hated to see where their government had forced us to live, but that only made them love and respect me even more.

My ninth-grade class in Switzerland. Nicole
is next to me, Livia in front of me.

Even with all the unfortunate circumstances, we couldn't have been happier with the life we had started in Switzerland. My mother, even though she was working a job she never thought she would, was happy to be able to provide a decent living for us. I continued to get good grades and dreamed of making a lot of money someday to help my mother out. Nothing gave me more pleasure than to see her face beaming with pride in me.

Mom and me at a park in Switzerland.

We still had no official word about my father, but also no shortage of speculation. Some claimed to have witnessed him leaving the concentration camp, others to have seen him being killed, and the Red Cross had no trace of him. Meanwhile, in a desperate attempt, my mother visited a psychic, who assured her that she saw my father in her visions and that he was still held captive.

With each day that passed, my mother's hopes for his return diminished, but I dreamed of him almost every night, and each time it was about our reunion: him smiling from ear to ear, lowering his knees, and extending his arms, and me running from across the street and leaping into them. I told myself that until I had physical proof of his death, I would never believe he was gone, and I'd forever hold out hope of jumping into his arms again.

CHAPTER 7

Nothing Good
Lasts Forever

OUR REFUGEE RESIDENCY STATUS IN Switzerland was temporary. To the best of our knowledge, Switzerland would allow
Bosnian refugees to stay for five years (while the war was on-
going) but reevaluate as needed based on resource constraints,
among other factors (age, level of trauma experienced in the
war, etc.). We were constantly reminded of that because every
six months my mother had to go to the local immigration
personnel at the police station to file for an extension of our
stay. And each time, it was a nerve-racking experience for her.
Not only were the personnel unfriendly, but they made her
and the other immigrants wait around for hours at a time.

I accompanied my mother a few times when I did not
have school obligations, but most of the time she went on her
own. Her German was decent enough for basic conversation,
but when it came to advanced communication, especially as it
related to laws and regulations, she needed help translating. It

just so happened that one time she went for the renewal, she was told to sign a new form, one that she did not fully understand. Being an immigrant, and not wanting to disobey any government personnel instructions for fear of being deported, she signed the form. Once I got home, she gave me the form to read and translate for her. I could not believe what I was reading. I reread it at least twice, and each time, there it was: my mother had agreed to leave Switzerland immediately, in exchange for ten thousand Swiss francs.

Turns out, the Swiss government was antsy to send Bosnians back to their home country. It had now been roughly a year since the official peace agreement ending the Bosnian War was forged in the United States in Dayton, Ohio, in December of 1995. While ceasefire was in effect on the ground, the country was far from being stable enough for refugees to return to their homes. Towns like ours had been leveled, and if we were to return, we would have to build a house first. This was where the Swiss incentive to return came into play. To them, ten thousand Swiss francs would be enough for us to get back on our feet and start living anew. To us, the country was just coming out of war, the economy was at a standstill, and neighbors who were once killing each other were now expected to live in peace again. The last thing we would think of was building a home there at this time. Yet it now appeared my mother and I were headed back "home" imminently.

That night, my mother did not sleep. I tried my best to comfort her, telling her that we would go back to the police station the next day and explain to them that she did not understand what she was signing. I believed someone had to realize that my mother was basically tricked into signing this serious form. At the very least, she should have been offered translation services. Instead, they had tacked this form at the end of the standard renewal process without fully explaining to her what it was, in hopes that they would get one more victim out of their system. I was furious, while my mother was scared to death.

I accompanied her to the police station the next day. The gentleman she'd interacted with the previous day was understanding to a certain point, yet made it clear that he was not in a position to reverse the form. We would have to appear at a hearing, present our case that we had no home to go back to, explain that we were afraid for our lives, and beg them to keep us in the country a little while longer.

The hearing took place before an immigration judge, and we were represented by a social worker. The judge decided that we were allowed to stay. But while we could breathe a sigh of relief for the moment, our respite was temporary—we were only given a year's extension before we had to depart. There was no way around it: we were going to have to leave Switzerland.

My mother frantically started calling various family members. Going back to Bosnia was simply not an option for us. Not only did we not have a place to go back to, but we did not feel safe returning there. Still having no official word about my father, the majority in our immediate family circle had concluded that he was dead, his remains lying somewhere in one of the many rumored mass graves. The last thing my mother wanted to do was put us in harm's way again with just the two of us alone in a deserted town. She wanted to find a permanent living option for us outside of Bosnia. She did not believe the country would recover quickly, and wanted to make sure that I had a chance at a better life.

At that time, the only two countries permanently taking in Bosnian refugees with open arms were the United States and Australia. While we knew some family members had already immigrated to Australia, being that far away from Europe would have been difficult for my mom, who was leaving her parents behind. So she decided to pursue the American route instead.

We had other family members who had immigrated to the United States as refugees through the Red Cross program. Our most immediate family member was my mom's aunt, who lived in Chicago with her family. After speaking to my mother over the phone, she submitted the paperwork for us to begin the "family reunion" immigration process.

At that time, the US government was allowing refugee families to be united from various parts of the world, and it processed those requests as quickly as possible. But getting through the initial immigration process was painful. First, we had to go through in-depth questioning by Immigration and Naturalization Services (INS) agents. For that, we had to travel to Germany (which meant we needed special permission from the Swiss government to leave and reenter the country) to a US base near Frankfurt, spend four hours under intense questioning (basically being interrogated), and return to Switzerland to await a response. The questioning was primarily used to determine eligibility for entry into the United States, to make sure we had no criminal activities in our past, and to determine that we were indeed persecuted refugees.

The agents wanted to hear every little detail of our journey following the onset of the Bosnian war. They even separated my mother and me for questioning and ultimately left us both crying profusely, having had to recount everything we had tried to forget over the past five years. Following a positive response from the INS, we would then have to redo all of our immunization and medical evaluations in Switzerland to determine that we were also physically and mentally healthy enough to enter the United States.

At last, the day came when my mother got the letter from the INS saying we were officially accepted into the United States as war refugees, under the condition of becoming permanent residents within nine months, with the option to become US citizens following an initial five-year permanent-resident status. Special arrangements were made for convoys of refugee families to travel all at once aboard a big plane headed toward New York before being dispersed among various American cities that had the necessary resources for housing, food, and so on. For us, that meant we would join the

July 1998 convoy (just before I would have to start a new school year), and our final destination was going to be the Greater Cincinnati area, just a mere half hour away from where the Bosnian peace agreement was negotiated. What a coincidence, I thought!

Meanwhile, I was dreading leaving Switzerland. I was angry at my mother for having gotten us into this situation. I was now sixteen years old, a raging teenager, and I did not want to leave the friendships I'd worked so hard to build over the years. While I had started to learn English at my school a year prior to our departure, my English was merely good enough for a tourist. I literally would have to start all over again, just like I had done in Switzerland, and I hated the thought of that.

All I knew about the United States was based on Hollywood movies and TV shows. In particular, I was a huge fan of *Beverly Hills, 90210*, which gave me hope that maybe there would be some coolness factor to this after all. At least my Swiss friends thought so. Everyone was jealous of my going to America. They dreamed of going there too someday and promised to come visit me.

While my friends dreamed of going to America, I day-dreamed during the remainder of the school year. For once, I left my foot off the educational gas pedal. If I had to start all over again anyway, why did it matter how I finished the year? I just wanted to enjoy the last few months I had with my friends. My last semester report card was tough to explain. It was an anomaly—a C average at best. Everyone was in shock at my grades. It was my last rebellious teenage act before we had to depart. Since I was being forced to leave a place I had come to love so much, I wanted it at least to be on my own terms, as a C student, which my mother hated.

CHAPTER 8

This Is Not *Beverly Hills, 90210*

THE LAST WEEK IN SWITZERLAND was emotionally charged for me. There were so many friends to say good-bye to. And each one of them, with their send-off presents and notes, made it even harder to swallow the fact that I had to leave. The only things that sweetened the good-byes were their promises to write me on a regular basis.

That same week, both of my mom's brothers and their families came to visit us from Slovenia before we had to depart. None of us knew when we would see each other again. We had never dreamed that we'd be continents apart. I shed tears on a daily basis, so much so that I didn't even recall packing the two checked bags I was allowed to bring with me. But there we were at the Zurich airport, with our family by our side, lugging four large suitcases and a big plastic bag with the INS logo prominently displayed on it. We had to carry that bag at all times so we were easily recognizable to the American authorities as refugees. My mother guarded that bag with her life! It was our lifeline, containing documents for a fresh new start and a promise for a permanent place to finally call home again.

My aunt making sure we had all of our documents
before we went to passport control.

After exchanging the last hugs, with tears running down uncontrollably, we passed through passport control and continued to wave back until we could not see our families' faces anymore.

July 28, 1998, was the first time we ever got on an airplane, an eight-hour journey to New York. The novelty of New York did not faze me that day. I kept thinking of the life I was leaving behind, my friends' faces flashing in front of my eyes, tears rolling down my cheeks as I remembered each one. My mother, being the everlasting optimist and survivor she was, tried to console me as much as she could. I did not understand it at the time, but now I know how torn apart she must have felt that day. On one hand she was on this journey to give us a chance at a better life, but on the other she was uprooting us again.

The eight-hour flight felt like an eternity, but we finally arrived in New York, only to be welcomed by rude immigration officers who shouted at us to get into the correct waiting line, which wrapped around the hall like a big snake. It wasn't until I learned about the stereotype of rude New Yorkers that I finally appreciated that moment for what it was. Standing in a line of refugees three rows wide, all clutching their big white plastic bags, I could not help but feel like we were cattle waiting to be sold.

Fifteen years later, as I was traveling for one of my international business trips and connecting through JFK, I spotted that same line of refugees in the immigration hall. I broke down in tears reliving that moment of my life. I wanted to tell them everything would be okay, and I called my mom for some comforting words.

We were assigned an "alien number," which became our new lifeline through the immigration process yet to come. With our fingerprints and "mug shots" officially in the database, we aliens were escorted out and pointed toward our connecting flight to Cincinnati.

Luckily, we had some family friends in the Greater Cincinnati area, people we had known back in Bosnia through my mom's side of the family. Just like my mom's aunt in Chicago, they had immigrated to the United States with the first batch of Bosnian war refugees. So once we got off the plane, we had about twenty Bosnians gathered around, finally welcoming us into this country.

I was exhausted, partly from crying and partly from the long journey, so I don't recall the drive to our new apartment. It was a small two-bedroom place with one bath and a kitchen that couldn't fit more than one person at a time, but to us it was a castle! Since we'd left Bosnia, we'd had to share everything but our bed with fellow refugees. Our new home was in the Pine Lake Apartments community in Florence, Kentucky, a small town just across the river from the city of Cincinnati, Ohio. A decent-sized Bosnian community was already established in northern Kentucky due to the industrial jobs there. I was told this particular apartment location was our best choice because it was assigned to Boone County High School, which had a good reputation, and four other Bosnians in the student body who could help me transition. I felt a small sense of relief thinking about the first day of school.

For the first time in six years, I finally had a room and a bed all to myself, and I enjoyed the most peaceful sleep I'd had in a while. When I awoke, it took me a moment to realize where I was. The only familiar thing was the scent of my mom's cooking, and I was starving. I was in no mood to talk, though, still angry at my mother for bringing me here, so we ate in silence.

A lot of paperwork was needed to be taken care of in order to start our new life, and, more importantly to her, for me to be able to start school on the first day, which was fast approaching. One of our Bosnian family friends took on the responsibility of helping us get around. The first order of business was to obtain a Social Security number (SSN). While our alien number was important from an immigration and legal status standpoint, we were told that nothing could ever get done in this country without a SSN. After we obtained the SSNs, we proceeded to the Health and Family Services offices, which would help us out financially (living stipend, food stamps, and Medicaid) for our first six months. On top of that, they enrolled my mother in an English language course, with the goal of finding her a job within those first six months.

The next stop was the school, to get me enrolled in classes for the coming year. After a lengthy debate with the principal over my records, and the alarmingly bad grades I'd gotten the last semester in Switzerland, it was decided that I would enter as a sophomore, but on a quick track to becoming a junior, simply due to the lack of my knowledge of the English language. In order to catch up, I would attend six months of intense English as a Second Language (ESL) classes, which would take up half of my school day. The other half would be spent in classes that wouldn't require much English, like algebra, geometry, and art.

I had roughly two weeks to get ready for school. Our family friend introduced me to three female Bosnian students attending the same school. All of them were friendly, but none were jumping at the idea of being my friend and helping me out. All of their families lived in a small apartment community right next door to Boone County High School, which allowed them to walk to school. Our parents decided that I would stay over at one of their apartments the night before the first day of school, and we would walk to school together. The thinking was that it would be easier for me not to walk into school all alone, and the girls would show me the way to my ESL classroom.

I felt nervous the night before, but I was confident I'd picked out the perfect outfit for the occasion. Having gotten into '90s hip-hop music while in Switzerland, I proudly laid out my clothes, Fila brand from head to toe: a brand-new white sweatshirt, navy-blue sweatpants, and white sneakers with blue soles. Coupled with the "cool" Eastpak backpack I'd brought with me from Switzerland, nothing was going to stand in my way. That is until the next day, when I caught the glances of my Bosnian friends, who wore summer dresses and sandals, and had their faces covered in makeup. Until I learned the correct English expression (something I still struggle with), I used to tell everyone that I was a "boyish girl". Now I know that I've been a tomboy all along.

The two-minute walk from their apartment to the school was the most anxious two minutes of my life. I had flashes of scenes from *Beverly Hills, 90210* run through my head. Would I see Dylan? What if Kelly sat next to me? I was sure if she did, Donna would be right there as well! But, Boone

County High School was no Beverly Hills High. With no fancy cars pulling into the parking lot, no big outdoor break area, and certainly no palm trees, it barely resembled what my image of a high school was. I was staring at what could only be described as a big concrete box on the side of a busy street. But my heart lifted when I saw the school buses blocking the front entrance. Finally, a familiar sight from the TV show—the big yellow school buses!

"Now that's cool," I whispered under my breath.

CHAPTER 9

I Never Thought I'd Hate Going to School

Upon entering the school, I immediately felt over-whelmed. The hallways were abuzz, rampant with activity. Like little bees, the students swarmed around me, bumping into me, rushing to find their classrooms before the first bell of the day. My Bosnian friends took me down one of the side hallways, pointed toward my ESL classroom, and then quickly disappeared for fear of being seen with me. The ESL classroom was isolated from the rest of the building and po-sitioned right next to the janitor's closet. At least it was quiet in that corner.

As I entered the room, an angel smiled down upon me— Ms. Farley, my ESL teacher. I sensed her comforting nature right away, and I was so relieved to be out of the hallway hustle and bustle that I just wanted to hug her. Ms. Farley introduced me to the rest of her students: two siblings from the Philippines and five kids from Mexico, who were related to one another. Each of them had varying levels of English knowledge, but everyone smiled at me and greeted me warmly. In an instant, I felt a strong connection to my ESL clan. They were going to be my saving grace.

My whole morning was spent one-on-one with Ms. Farley, who was trying to gauge how good my English was in order to create a learning plan specific to my needs. Then the bell rang, and it was time for lunch. Ms. Farley had the other ESL students show me the way to the cafeteria, and they were kind enough to sit with me that day. But our interaction was limited. For the most part, we just smiled at one another while eating our pizza.

Following lunch was my geometry class, and I left the cafeteria early enough to find the classroom in time. As I opened the door, everyone in the room got quiet, turned around, and stared at me. I lowered my head and proceeded to the first open seat I noticed. It was in front of a big, bulky guy, who I later learned was the captain of the football team and the chief school bully. I kept my head down, not making any eye contact, and waited for the teacher, with my pencil ready to go. She was running a few minutes late, and I couldn't have been happier once she started the lesson. As I feverishly copied down her notes from the chalkboard, I could hear a lot of giggling and commotion behind my back. But no way was I turning around to see what was going on.

I powered through that class, and the rest of the day was one big blur as I made my way from classroom to classroom, always keeping my head down, hoping nobody would say anything to me, as I wouldn't have known how to respond.

When the final bell rang, it was time to make my way to the school bus line and head home. I was excited to finally get a chance to ride on one of these "famous" buses, but I wasn't sure which was the right one. Luckily, I found an attendant and mumbled, "Pine Lake Apartments," and he pointed me to the correct bus.

The elderly man sitting behind the wheel was the friendliest face I would ever encounter on that bus. Each of the other kids occupied a bench to themselves; nobody made space for me to sit but just silently watched me walk by. I squeezed my way into the very last row, and the other students moved away from me. Tears were starting to form, so I took a few deep breaths and told myself not to cry as I stared out the window. As the bus made its way from home to home, I made note of my surroundings, and everything felt so strange. How could I ever feel at home here?

I dropped on the couch when I finally got to our apartment. My mother was so anxious to hear about my day, but all I wanted to do was cry. It only made matters worse when she asked me what was on the back of my sweatshirt. My brand-new white Fila sweatshirt was plastered with a big blue piece of gum that had etched itself into the material over the course of the day. The commotion behind my back during geometry class finally made sense: the captain of the football team had disposed of his gum onto my sweatshirt. As I burst into tears, my mother rushed to get the sweatshirt off me to "fix it." But I knew it would never be the same.

Day in and day out, I endured similar torturous days in high school. I said many times before that I had endured being in a war zone, but high school felt way worse at that time. Outside of the ESL classroom walls, I said little and kept to myself. Most days I ate lunch alone, and I felt embarrassed when I had to give the cafeteria lady the code that allowed me to get a free lunch due to my mother and me being on welfare.

Because of my misery at school, my mother's days weren't easy either. I became so angry that one day I packed up my suitcase and headed for the front door. I had a little bit of allowance money saved up that I was going to use for a one-way ticket back to Switzerland. She ran after me into the hallway and, with tears in her eyes, begged me to come back inside. Lots of phone calls were made to my grandmother in Switzerland. She did her best to try and calm me down, since I was still angry at my mother.

The only solace was the time I'd spend on the weekends with one of my younger Bosnian friends, Nataša, who was in middle school at that time and not yet afraid to associate with me. The rest of the Bosnian girls didn't want to risk their hard-earned clique status in high school. They would smile and acknowledge me while in my presence, but they wouldn't spend more than a few minutes chit-chatting with me. And God forbid we speak Bosnian in the hallways. Being different was not acceptable in high school; one had to find a way to fit in, and I understood their situation.

After only six months in, Ms. Farley felt confident enough in my English that she petitioned for me to attend all of the regular classes. I was confident in it too, even though I didn't say much. The straight A's in all of my classes were sufficient enough. But even though I was back to excelling in school, I hated every moment of it. The thing that I had loved so much since childhood became the thing I dreaded every morning. So I became determined to make something out of myself without the need for school.

All my Bosnian schoolmates were working part-time jobs, mostly to help support their families' blue-collar earnings. One of them helped me get a job too, and soon I was a proud Winn-Dixie cashier. The pay was not bad for a seventeen-year-old student, and I devoted any free time I had to working at the store. Interacting with adults was much more pleasant than dealing with the kids at school. I had regular weekly customers who grew to love me and would wait around just to pass through my line. My favorite was an elderly couple who always came to the store on the same day at the same time and always bought the same things. They were quite particular about how their groceries were bagged too, and I happily obliged them. This proved to be a winning recipe, as I was quickly promoted to work at the customer service desk.

With a nice sum of money to my name and an environment that was friendly to me, I proclaimed to my mother one day that I would not continue going to school after I finished high school. Even though she had never stood in the way of anything

I ever wanted and always tried to please me, this idea was not well received. Much to my surprise, she exclaimed that it was unacceptable and that she was not having this conversation with me. I was going to college whether I liked it or not. In her own words, I was not going to end up working a menial job like she was forced to do. No. She'd worked so hard to bring me to this country, and her daughter was going to make something of herself. And with the fast track I was put on, following my junior year, at age eighteen, I attended summer school classes to obtain my credit for English 4, which was the only thing standing in my way of a high school diploma and attending college. I was in a classroom with a handful of seniors from various local schools who had flunked English 4, and the only one with plans of going to college following summer school.

I graduated at the end of that summer, receiving my diploma at an ad hoc graduation ceremony attended by the Boone County High School principal himself, Mr. Sanders. My mother sat in the front row alongside all our Bosnian friends, tears in her eyes. Mr. Sanders was the only one to show up from the various other schools that had students graduating that day. And he didn't just show up; he'd prepared a speech just for me, highlighting the struggles I had endured in order to be where I was that day. As I walked up to the podium to shake his hand and obtain my diploma, I was overcome with emotion, and tears started to roll down my cheeks—happy tears. I was surrounded by my Bosnian refugee family, closing another painful chapter in my life, and looking forward to what Northern Kentucky University (NKU) had in store for me.

Me walking down in tears after accepting my high school diploma.

Mr. Sanders, Mom, and me at the high school graduation ceremony.

Me celebrating my high school graduation.

CHAPTER 10

The "Cool Kid" on Campus

I ONLY HAD A FEW weeks in between my summer high school graduation and my first semester at NKU. We chose NKU primarily due to the low tuition cost, but we also liked that it was a small enough university that I wouldn't get lost in the shuffle and could have easy access to the professors while I continued to perfect my English. Plus, it was close to home so I could commute, which was important for my mother.

We attended an orientation session, and somehow in my admission paperwork, my major was declared as business management (I blame the language barrier). Upon reading a bit more about it, I quickly decided management wasn't the right major for me. It felt too limiting. Growing up, I'd always thought I'd follow in my father's footsteps and end up working in a hospital. However, having witnessed the horrors of war, to this day I have trouble going inside a hospital, seeing blood or needles, or even breathing in that hospital scent, which I associate with death (leave it to the irony of life that my better half just happens to be a doctor, working in a hospital).

If medicine wasn't for me, my culture regarded a business degree as the next best thing. As I reviewed the rest of the business majors available to me, the only one that caught my attention was the marketing degree. When we finished meeting with the advisor in the school of business, the paperwork was submitted to officially switch my major. I'm so happy I did, as that allowed me to cross paths with Dr. Levin, a marketing professor and a market research advocate who became my lifelong mentor and someone to whom I owe my start in a now fourteen-year career in the marketing research industry.

Unlike when I began high school, I started college at the same time as my peers, and we were all in the same unfamiliar boat. Luckily for us, NKU had a class specifically to help freshmen get oriented to college life, and I happily signed up for University 101. This worked out particularly well for me, given that I had graduated as an "in-between years" student, and there weren't a lot of familiar high school faces to encounter on campus. Besides, most of my Boone classmates had chosen to either move away from home or not attend college at all. Years later, I spotted the captain of the football team, the one who'd loved to bully me, serving drinks at the local Applebee's.

For the first time since I left Bosnia, I felt like I had a fresh start in school and was no longer an outsider. On top of that, the students I encountered in college were much more open minded than the students I had encountered in high school. Anytime my name was called, it sparked intrigue, and for the most part, the other students were eager to hear about my story. And one day, during my first semester as a sophomore, I was approached by someone from the campus newspaper staff, asking to do a story on me. Soon, there I was on the front page of *The Northerner*, with a bold headline: "Bosnian Refugee Finds Peace on Campus." Who knew that I would become one of the "cool kids" in school? I finally started to feel at ease living in this country.

Picture of the original *Northerner* article,
which my mom still has in her files.

Our immigration status had changed in the meantime as well. Following our initial nine-month probationary period, we were allowed to apply for permanent resident status, also known as the green card. This meant that we were allowed to leave and reenter the country anytime we wished, because this was now our permanent home. Nobody was more excited about that than my mother. She was tired of having to move us from place to place, and she vowed never to leave Florence, Kentucky. I was excited about it too, but only because it meant I could travel back to Europe and reunite with the friends and family I'd left behind.

Every summer break, I left for the maximum allowable time (three months) and spent it in Switzerland at my grand-mother's. Visiting there for months at a time made me feel as if I were still living there. And because everyone was off for the summer, I saw all of my former friends from school, and each year we resumed our friendships without skipping a beat. Most of them were still writing to me on a regular basis. They still thought it was so cool that I lived in the United States, but nobody had the means to come and visit me yet. We brainstormed ways to get me to come back and live in Switzerland. One sure way was to obtain my college degree and US citizenship, and then move back there for a job. And that became my dream.

As I dreamed of moving back to Switzerland, my moth-er dreamed of me staying in the United States by her side. Over the years, my mother and I grew very close. While she always played the nurturing mother role, she also became my best friend. As I gained and lost friends over the years, she was always there, reminding me that a mother's love and friendship is sincere and selfless. And even though we've butted heads many times, I'm conscious she's the one who gave life to me, over and over again when life seemed to be pointless. Yet, she revealed to me recently that I've been the driving force behind her, that without me she wouldn't have had a reason to go on and fight for a better life for us. Today, it's very clear to both of us that we needed each other.

While I contemplated leaving the United States, she used to tell me we had come all this way together; we should never separate. And why would you want to leave this place? she would ask. The United States had given us a chance to have a normal life again. It propped us up when we needed it the most, gave us a chance to acclimate, and now we were truly a part of this society, fully integrated, self-sufficient, and productive. For my mother, there was no other place to call home. The United States was our home and she had no intentions of ever leaving it.

It would take me a few more years to mature and finally understand her point of view. But I did jump at the first opportunity to apply for US citizenship, regardless of whether I decided to leave or stay. Immigration rules required you to be a resident of this country for at least four years and nine months prior to having a right to apply for citizenship. And the process wasn't easy, quick, or cheap.

First, the application fee alone was $320 at that time (and the fee has more than doubled since then). Then, a thorough background check was performed. Following that, you had to pass a citizenship test. The government sent you a booklet containing all sorts of information about US history, and you could be tested on any of it. The test questions might ask anything from who the president was in a given year to how many congressional representatives your state had or how the voting process worked. On top of that, you were required to write an essay on a random open-ended question. That alone caused my mother panic; her English writing skills weren't as good as her speaking skills, since she hadn't had a chance to attend formal school here. That's why she didn't apply at the same time as I did, and she practiced a bit more with the study booklet.

Finally, the day came when I was to be sworn in as a US citizen. But first the immigration officer offered me a free one-time name change, courtesy of the US government. After my initial decline, he pressed on by giving me "beautiful American names" as an incentive—Miranda, Marissa, or perhaps Melissa. To him, everything was a better alternative than Mirsada. But nothing could induce me to change the name my father had given me. It was the last symbol of my heritage, as I was signing away my Bosnian citizenship rights in order to become an American citizen.

My mom at her US citizenship ceremony.

CHAPTER 11

America, My New Home

THE DAY I BECAME AN American citizen, I wondered what my father would have thought of us being in the United States. I remember sitting with him in the car, listening to the political talk shows right before the war officially broke out. Even though I didn't understand the politics behind it, I do recall my father talking about Bill Clinton and the rest of the Western world, which, he was convinced, would intervene any day now and save us from tyranny. While the West did eventually intervene, it was too late to save my father and more than one hundred thousand other Bosnians. Just as I was getting ready to graduate from college in 2004, his remains were discovered in a mass grave near the last concentration camp he was in, along with more than forty other brutally tortured and murdered men.

Over the years, we heard from eyewitnesses, including my dad's father, that my dad was one of the most tortured prisoners inside the camp. He was so abused that when my grandfather encountered him in the camp, he did not recognize this battered and bruised individual as his son.

He told my grandfather, "Say hello to my girls. I don't think I'm getting out of here alive."

My father endured months of torture, even was moved from the Keraterm concentration camp to another called Omarska, a more deadly one, where very few men made it out alive. My father ultimately succumbed there to his oppressors. One of his cousins, Enes, was held prisoner there as well. He was one of the lucky ones to survive it, and in December of 2015, as I sat on his couch in Germany, he told me, with tears in his eyes, the story of the last time he saw my father alive. It was something he knew he would have to do someday as his duty to my father and to me.

They were sitting on the concrete floor, Enes said, the room overcrowded and hot, when he saw my father slowly get up and head for the door. Being that the prisoners were not allowed to make any moves without being instructed to do so, two of the armed soldiers immediately took note of my father and asked him what he was doing. My father was silent and kept walking toward the door. At that point one of the soldiers hit him in the face with a rifle. My father's once-sturdy frame, now weak and malnourished, crumpled to the ground, and the two soldiers dragged him outside into the courtyard. Like the rest of the prisoners, my father was exhausted; he hadn't eaten a full meal since he'd been captured. When they yelled at him to get up off the ground, he couldn't rise quickly enough, so one of the soldiers shot him in the kneecap. He let out a shriek, but pain was irrelevant at that point.

As his cousin recollects, my father had reached a point of no return. The months of daily physical and mental torture had broken him down. He did not feel pain anymore; he just wanted his misery to be over. After they commanded him a few more times to get up, and he couldn't do so, they shot him in the other kneecap. My father collapsed to the ground and let out one last scream. His cousin remembers hearing two more shots, and then all was silent. My father's misery was finally over.

I now had proof of my father's murder, and I needed to accept the fact that he was indeed gone forever. However, it would take me eight more years to muster the courage to head back to Bosnia. At age thirty, twenty years after we were forced to flee our home, I made a symbolic trip back to my homeland. I organized a memorial service at the local mosque and finally said good-bye to my dad at his grave. I also got an opportunity to see some family members I hadn't seen since we were dispersed to different countries around the world.

My cousin Senada was there all the way from Austria. She used to be my swimming partner, but now she was holding her daughter Melina, whom I was meeting for the first time. Unlike me, she still didn't have an official word on her dad's whereabouts. He lay buried in one of the many mass graves still waiting to be unearthed in Bosnia. And my dad's cousin Midho was also there, the one who'd been picked up the same day as my dad, only to be released because his name wasn't on the list. I was happy to see that he was still alive. My dad's brother Abaz was in attendance too. He was the one who'd taken ownership of my dad's remains following the discovery in the mass grave. As his duty to me, he presented me with copies of all the documentation of my dad's exhumation. That day was bittersweet, but it was the closure I needed to finally accept my past.

Me at my dad's grave for the first time.

Given that I was only ten years old when we left Bosnia, I never even had a chance to get to know my homeland. After an emotional three-day visit in my hometown, I went on a week-long tour of the rest of Bosnia, visiting major cities along the way. Everywhere I went, ruins—scars from the war—were still visible to the eye and painful to digest. This beautiful country, a gem of the Balkans, ravaged by war so many times in its history, was still trying to recover. Yet with a forced peace agreement and its inhabitants divided, Bosnia hasn't been the same since, and perhaps it never will be. What remains unchanged are the people whose spirits cannot be broken. People who are survivors, fighters until their last breath—and I felt proud to be one of them.

Sitting on the plane headed back to the United States, I felt for the first time like I was going home. Today, I know and accept the fact that my life wouldn't be what it is had it not been for the war. The war is a piece of my life puzzle. Being a refugee is another. Like everyone else, I have many different pieces in my puzzle. Nonetheless, we are all members of the human race, and we all face struggles along this journey we call life. Struggle is a vital part of our lives; all we need is courage to keep us moving forward.

Closing Thoughts

ACCORDING TO THE OFFICIAL DOCUMENTS, the Bosnian War lasted three years, eight months, one week, and six days until the peace agreement was signed on December 14, 1995. Since then, it has been estimated that over one hundred thousand innocent lives were cut short, representing roughly one quarter of the total Bosnian population in 1992. Close to twenty thousand women were raped. And over two million people were forced to flee their homes (many of whom, myself included, are still living in countries outside of Bosnia). Over thirty thousand people were reported missing after the war. Many of them have since been uncovered in hundreds of mass graves all over Bosnia, but estimates show more than six thousand are still missing today, twenty-three years after the war ended. The war marked the biggest ethnic cleansing / genocide and displacement of people in Europe since World War II.

In 1993, the United Nations created an ad hoc court, the International Criminal Tribunal, located in the Hague (the

Netherlands) and responsible for prosecuting those who were in charge of the crimes committed in Bosnia. The court was dissolved as of December 31, 2017. During its twenty-four-year tenure, the court indicted one hundred sixty-one individuals. Ninety were convicted, twenty-one acquitted, and thirteen had cases transferred to other countries. Another thirty-seven had their cases terminated either due to death or lack of evidence. While the attempt to bring these individuals to justice has been a noble one, you will find hardly any Bosnians who feel that justice has been served, especially those who still don't know where their loved ones lie buried (like my cousin Senada).

There are still way too many open wounds. The country is divided to this day, territory-wise and in terms of its political future. The economy has been sputtering at best. The war left most of the infrastructure in ruins, and it is still being rebuilt. As a result, most of the young workforce has left the country in pursuit of a chance at a better life for their families. The majority of those who still live in Bosnia are elderly men and women who don't want to leave their homeland. Those of us living outside the country infuse the economy with cash when we visit during the few months of our summer or winter vacations, and then the economy stagnates until we return again. I fear that the country will eventually end up in war once more, but my hope is that we can find common ground before that occurs. War is never a solution. Innocent people will always be the sole victims. And for what?

My journey as a refugee began at age ten. I did not have a permanent place to call home again until age sixteen, when I arrived in the United States. I've seen too many dead bodies, witnessed too much human anguish, and suffered persecution in various parts of the world. Yet I'm happy to be alive and well today. Isn't that what every human being wants, after all? As I reflected on my thirty-fifth year of being on this planet, I wrote a poem titled "Life," which I will leave you with.

Life

⤳

AT SOME POINT OR ANOTHER, most of us question its meaning,
Trying to find greater purpose behind our existence.
And yet we didn't choose life;
Someone else made that choice for us.
But here we are…living, breathing, searching.

Some of us came into this world under favorable circumstances;
Others haven't fared as well.
Whatever the case may be, we've all felt the waves of life
crashing ashore.
Some bigger than others,
Some more powerful than others,
Some smoother than others.

And so we sit in the water,
Like a surfer on a windy day,
Waiting for that next wave.
Hoping we catch it at the right time,
Rise above it,
And ride it out as long as we can…mastering it along the way.

Maybe that is the point of it all…in this sea of life.

ABOUT THE AUTHOR

_⟶_

MIRSADA KADIRIC WROTE THIS BOOK at age thirty-six, twenty years after her arrival in the United States. After a few brief stints living in Ohio, she is back to calling home the state that initially welcomed her to this country, Kentucky. She obtained her bachelor of science in marketing in 2004 and went back to Northern Kentucky University for her master's in business administration, which she completed in 2009. NKU continues to be near and dear to her heart, and in 2012 she was recognized as NKU's Outstanding Young Researcher of the Decade (thanks to her mentor, Dr. Levin). She is currently employed at Kao USA, Inc. as a senior manager of market research for the global John Frieda brand. She and her boss have a running joke that they're helping save the world one shampoo at a time.

In her free time, Mirsada loves to explore the world, checking off cities and countries on her long travel wish list. She still makes time to visit Switzerland at least once every year to see her grandmother, who still resides there. Her mother lives within a ten-minute drive from her, and Mirsada couldn't be happier about that. A good homemade Bosnian meal will brighten any bad day.

As of January 2018, Mirsada is also serving as president of the board for a local nonprofit organization called RefugeeConnect, which is dedicated to empowering refugees to be a part of the Greater Cincinnati community. Further, she volunteers as a mentor to two teenage refugee girls, one from Syria and the other from Eritrea, at Withrow High School. The one thing Mirsada lacked during her initial years in the United States was a mentor while she was in high school, and she couldn't be more eager to help these young refugees have an easier transition to their new life in the United States.

Writing will continue to be a hobby for Mirsada, who hopes to publish more of her reflections in the years to come.